GW00384615

TIDAL I
Ebb and Flow in Appledore

Nigel Melville

With a foreword
by
Tom Andrews

FOR SUE

ODUN BOOKS
Appledore, North Devon EX39 1PT

FOREWORD

One of the things most likely to aggravate any locally born person is the stranger who comes to the area, picks a few brains, reads back issues of local newspapers and a random selection of local topographical books; then proceeds to "write" his own book in a plagiaristic way – and overnight becomes an authority on almost anything local.

Myself, being little different from most locals (having been born and bred in Appledore, my forebears probably having eaten missionaries), have an inbred suspicion of "bliddy furriners" who come to take rather than give. Sometimes, however, one's attitude is changed.

It has been my good fortune to have known Nigel Melville for some seventeen years. Initial acquaintance started through a common interest in Adult Education, developing over the years to a firm friendship. He has, to use local vernacular, "served his time" in the area before putting this intriguing book together. Timely produced, both informative and entertaining, full of the yesterdays and todays of Appledore, it has much appeal and is in my opinion very readable, and unique.

I wish it the luck it deserves and commend it to both furriners and locals alike.

TOM ANDREWS

~~~~~~~~~~~~~~~~~~~~~~~~~~

ISBN 1 873129 00 9

CONTENTS

INTRODUCTION

This isn't a history book, nor is it a guide book. I am not qualified by scholarship to write the first, or by lifelong residence to write the second. I have lived in North Devon, though, for seventeen years and in Appledore for the last six of them, which - I hope - qualifies me to put down my appreciation of an underestimated village in a few scribbled sketches.

A lot of people who visit Appledore drive down the hill (as I did when I first came here), shudder a little at the crude old crane looming over the blind wall that leads to the river's edge, swing round the corner to the quay, and start leaving the village past the church before realising that it has come to an end and that they are on the narrow road that leads to Westward Ho!

On that first visit, I wondered what had put Appledore in the guide books, and why such an apparently colourless little spot had such a lovely name.

It took several more visits, on foot, around Market Street and Irsha Street, before I learned what I had been missing. Even so, I lived here for months - slipping in and out of hidden courts, sitting and watching the riverside scene at the Quay, meeting the people who sailed boats for pleasure or business, and coming out of my front door in Bude Street to the astonishing sight of a coastal dredger apparently crossing the road just below my house - before I really began to grasp what an extraordinary little place this is.

When my wife and I moved to another house in the village and discovered that we had bought a field and three stables, we began to take Appledore's hidden realities rather more seriously.

Vernon Boyle began his chapter on Appledore in *Devon Harbours* with the uncompromising words "I am sorry to say that Appledore is the place where they eat the missionaries - or so Bideford people allege." I hope those days have long gone (though Boyle wrote that as recently as 1952 and one local says they would still eat missionaries, but can't get them so easily now), but I acknowledge that Appledore people, however welcoming they are to visitors, are a race apart. That said, I can only offer Robert Burns' warning -

"A chield's amang you taking notes,
and, faith, he'll prent it."

and hope for the best. If I have maligned anyone, I apologise. If I have left out anything vital, there could always be a larger second edition. I rather hope there will.

Nigel Melville

RISING TIDE

Dawn view above Odun Farm

Dawn and sunrise are two different things when you are an animal or a bird.   Long before the sky lightens enough to silhouette the trees, Hamish has told everybody to welcome the new day.   Hamish is an orphan cockerel; not the sort of creature you expect to hear in the crowded centre of a fishing community, but Appledore is not the sort of place where things are always as you expect them to be.   Hamish is an orphan because he arrived in a sack from a battery farm, brought by a soft-hearted feed-lorry driver who thought he deserved a better future than a close encounter with a dinner table.

Come to think of it, Hamish doesn't really welcome the day; he lets out a cry of frustration and anger, possibly because the light has gone on in the chicken shed to encourage his harem to get down to the serious business of laying eggs.

Outside, it is still dark, even in the summer, for the time is not yet 5.00 in the morning.   Wait and watch.   In time, the tops of the trees will begin to stand out a little from the sky, and over Tapeley Park the steel grey begins to become deep purple and later magenta.

Below you, the mud flats turn to pale lilac and the water takes on the colour of the sky, but with the sheen of burnished metal.   The tide is coming towards the full, and the bows of the yachts on swinging moorings are headed out to sea.   To the right, where there is still not a domestic light to be seen, the outlines of the houses in Tomouth slowly remove the illusion that you are on the open hills that once flowed down to a creek by an empty river.

In one place alone is there the slightest sign of life. The glove factory in New Street never closes, and the metallic slithering of the machines rattles on day and night.

Time was when the hooters would begin to sound about now in the Richmond ship repair yard, but that was a few years ago, and it wants an hour yet before the Bidna men leave their breakfasts to cycle off to work.

Things are changing in Appledore, as they always have; sometimes for the better, more often - according to some of the locals - for the worse. The rising sun makes things a little clearer as the day begins, but nothing can make the future of the village any clearer.

From the hillside above Odun Road and below the suburban tidiness of Yeo Drive or Staddon Road, there is not enough light at this time of the morning to show up the changes that have happened around Appledore. The bulk of Richmond House looms darker against a dark sky, and you needn't know that the shipbuilder's mansion is now divided into flats. Staddon still lurks behind its protective trees, larger now than when they were first planted round the house 150 years ago. The backs of the houses in Odun Road haven't changed at all in a century, and as the sun lightens the river from steel to silver, Tapeley House over at Westleigh can be seen looking across the river to Knapp House as it did in the days of the iniquitous Thomas Benson.

Only when the sun actually breaks the horizon will the spell be broken. The estate at Tomouth takes the place of the rough grazing above the old creek, into which was built the Richmond Dock. The houses behind you rise from the fields of the old farm. Across the estuary, the squat bulk of the abandoned power station becomes a silhouette blocking the view of the RAF base. At least, it still hunched over the mudflats in mid-1989 when I first drafted these essays, but its bulk grew smaller as the demolition men moved through the vast empty hall.

In the centre of Instow, the shape that might have been the Marine Hotel is seen to be more modern flats, the railway line that passes the old signal box reveals its trackless state, the additions to the house that became the Commodore Hotel become more plain and the Jubilee Hall, once the entertainment Mecca of Instow, is revealed to have become the Lobster Pot and the Boat House.

But all that is no more than the light cast by the sun, and the boats rise to a tide that comes in every twelve hours. Another twelve hours and the sun will have gone again; another six, and the tide will be out once more. Things come and they go again. Appledore is not what it was, and it isn't what it will be, and the tide which takes all manner of objects out to sea may well bring some of them back again on its return.

That is part of the mystery of Appledore. I don't say "charm", for that is far too genteel a word for a place where people still earn a hard living by making boats and by working them on a sea that has always demanded respect. Somewhere inside the present village and its activities are the remains of what went before – the harrying of the Danes, the building of wooden ships from Tudor to Victorian days (they say it was an Appledore man who hoisted Nelson's "England expects ...." at Trafalgar), the smuggling and the transatlantic trade, the fishing and the poaching, the making of ropes, sails, shirts and gloves, and the Victorian ventures in to the early years of technology. It's all still there, if you only know where to look.

HIGH WATER

Start of the day
at the Lifeboat Slip

The tide is as high as it can be, down here where the river almost meets the sea. "Almost", but not quite, for the meeting point is out there at the bar, passable now and for a couple of hours or so either side of high water, and a turbulent mess of surf and shallows at all other times.

There has been a lifeboat here for over 150 years, for the lifeboat house dates back to 1825, and the rolls of honour on its walls listing the rescues (or "services" as the RNLI so diffidently calls them) have the gilded dignity of scholarship lists in public school halls. Back in 1952, Vernon Boyle was describing a recent service when he wrote of –

> "... the scene when in 1949 they took this Lifeboat out over the Bar at dead low water in a living gale, her bottom scraping the sand when she was in the trough, to go to the wreck of the *Monte Gurugu*; or that when in 1945 she took seven men off a concrete blockship which was adrift in the Channel thirty miles away. For us who live here there are many Lifeboat memories as stirring; one for each year of our life.
>
> Sixty years ago the Appledore men had three Lifeboats at the same time situated miles apart. To one, on the North Side they had to go out in boats across the Estuary. Those Lifeboats were surf-boats, and there was one on each side of the Bar. The one on the south, at the north point of Northam

Burrows, was housed amongst sand hills and had to go down over the Pebble Ridge on a great carriage hauled by farm horses. I saw it launched once, about the year 1898. The horses were out in the sea, breasting the breakers. They were led by Lion, a noble beast. The horses were led in a curve to face the land, so the Lifeboat could slide off and head seawards. One man I saw had his hand streaming with blood; another there, the old cox'n, had before that been swept overboard and dragged in again by the yoke-lines, in which he had luckily got entangled. Nothing at sea or on the battlefield can outmatch the stories of our Lifeboats."

The "noble beasts" grazed their off-duty hours in a field on the edge of West Appledore. As soon as the maroon was fired, alerting the village to a lifeboat service, the horses became excited and, as soon as their gate was opened would gallop out on to the Burrows and be waiting ready to be harnessed to the launching trolley by the time the crew had arrived.

Boyle's "one for each year of our life" is plain fact: over 450 lives saved in the last 160-odd years, over 60 shipwrecks in the first sixty years of the 19th century. Those silver and bronze RNLI medals were not easily won.

Legend has it that once you laid hands on an oilskin you were automatically a member of the lifeboat crew for that rescue. The story goes that a man had arrived at the lifeboat house and had donned his oilskin and was awaiting his brother when another man arrived intent on getting an oilskin. As he put hand on the hanging jacket a knife flashed and he had lost a finger. The honour of serving the lifeboat was not easily granted.

~~~~~~~~~~

The old granite slip looks fit to stand up to anything the sea can throw at it; and it needs to. Once, when trying foolishly to bring my sloop "Snowdrift" up on to its road trailer here at half-tide I ventured the thought that the swell might become gentler as the tide rose. It didn't, and next season, when I first rowed a new 'pram' to the slip, one wave carried me over the slip and on to the rocks beyond, and when I scrambled out the next one lifted the pram, all six foot of marine ply, clean over my head. Back on the quay the tourists were all saying what a lovely calm start-of-summer day it was.

We are less than a mile from that quay, but we could be in a different climate completely. When the wind is in the west, there is nothing to block the Atlantic gales, and the cross-currents fight each other around the miniature cliffs below the old Custom House. (Well, they call it the "old" Customs House, but that's only because it is older than the new one; the original Customs House was where you would expect it to be, on the corner of the Quay.) Anyway, if the wind has veered at all to the north, the waves will be over the seawalls and into the bungalow gardens.

It isn't always violent here, but it is never predictable. One summer day, we spent almost the whole day down here sunbathing and paddling, for everything a small boy needs for afternoon entertainment is here. As the tide came in, our motor cruiser "Susan V" lifted off the sand, and we set out for an end-of-day excursion into the estuary. Over by Crow, the current ran too fast for our anchor, and when we watched some of the open boats running fast for their moorings with neither engine, sails or oars to speed them faster than the current, we settled for a river cruise instead. Minutes later, we were upstream from the Quay.

The sky that had been a cloudless blue suddenly turned an angry yellow, and the light and the fun went out of the day. We turned back towards the lifeboat slip, but as we motored past the Quay, the fog was rolled out over the river like a felt carpet underlay and much the

13

same colour. By the time we were opposite the Seagate, we could see no more than 40 or 50 feet, and the only way home was by the sort of navigation aid that features in no nautical almanac - "that's the green two-master, so John's boat is ahead about 20 yards: Cyril's is as far again, but a bit to the right. From there, we ought to be able to see the lifeboat."

Indeed, we saw the lifeboat, and swung to port a little, as I usually did in better weather. Within a second or two we could begin to follow the noise of the waves on the rocks below where the cannon once sounded for pre-war regattas.

Once on the mooring, we began the process of off-loading luggage and family in a leaky and elderly two-seater inflatable. The first maroon went off as my stepson and the picnic gear were landed. Warning him that a second maroon might follow, I returned for my wife, the towels and the swimming kit, pushing off just as the second maroon headed skywards.

Before we were back at the slip, the inshore boat was on its way out to sea, and it was suddenly rather a frightening evening. Later, we heard that both lifeboats had been out and towed a queue of half a dozen lost yachts back to safety.

~~~~~~~~~~

It was at this same slip that "Susan V" met her end - twice. It is not given to every boat to be wrecked twice, and to manage it in the same small sideway of the sea is something of an achievement.

The first foundering began before breakfast with a panting phone call from a friend. She was on the rocks, and if I were quick, I *might* save the engine. Armed with spanners and ropes, I drove to the slip. Sure enough, she was on the rocks, but jammed firmly against the side of the slip and lifting slightly on the swell.

It took almost an hour, waist-deep in cold October water, to remove the outboard before an elderly fisherman was able to hoist it on to the slip. Another hour in the rising tide, and "Susan V" was free of the rocks, from where we were able to float her on to the slip. The lifeboat tractor towed her up on to dry land, and the crew of locals who had gathered to watch the fun manhandled her on to the trailer.

Nine months later, repaired and nearly watertight, she was back at the slip and on the market. Warned that final repairs still needed to be done, her new owner took her out for a fishing cruise to Morte and presented us with some of the catch before, so I thought, taking her out of the water.

A week or so later, I was puzzled to see her still at her mooring and sitting a little low in the water. A week after that, driving past the slip at high water, I was relieved to see that the moorings were vacant. Then I noticed the white rod sticking up out of the water – the tip of the aerial that I had never actually connected to a radio. A fortnight after that, I heard that she had broken up in a gale, less than 20 yards from where she had first gone aground.

~~~~~~~~~~

Look out to sea. The tracking skills of the bushman and the American Indian baffle the western mind. In much the same way, the seafarer's skill on the water baffles the landsman. To the casual eye, this is just a lot of water at high tide, and a lot less at low; but Vernon Boyle and every Appledore seafarer knows better –

> "Every diminutive point or bight or heap of stones or mussel bed has its name, and very strange names some of them are. Here is Shar's Hook (Chardellhoke in 1609), here is Mally Mounzel, this is Hart Weir, this is the Tallet, and that the Pulleys, Klondike

is the name given fifty years ago to a bank of gravel by the South Tail where barge-owners made fortunes, and Old Walls below the lighthouse is a place where three salmon boats can fish at once. All these places and dozens more can be seen from pretty well every house in West Appledore. The name Pulleys is important; for instance, there are two buoys named the Inner and Outer Pulleys, out there towards Bar. The word Pulleys means "Pools with big pebbles" and there are a good many pulleys here, especially on the west bank of the estuary."

And the prosaic Admiralty chart has a word of warning to any casual yachtsman who tries to slip over the Bar at the last minute –

CAUTION – CHANGING DEPTHS AND AIDS

The bar and sands are constantly shifting and the buoys are occasionally moved to allow for this. Frequent changes in depths may be expected in the River Torridge above Appledore. The course and depth of the River Taw between Fremington Pill and Barnstaple are subject to daily change.

No wonder a pilot boat with a luridly fluorescent orange topside runs out to meet every vessel of any size that ventures over the Bar. No wonder, either, that lawyers can earn a lot of money out of the ambiguities of pilotage and salvage.

~~~~~~~~~

Facing the sea by the slip are two customs houses, both now turned over to the new demands of holiday travellers. The older one is by far the larger, appropriately enough for the long gone years when Bideford was one of the largest importers of tobacco, when new import duties suddenly made the weed an attractive cargo for the free-traders, and a demanding job for the two officers and their boatman who had to keep the King's eye on the channel and its traffic.

The free trade was attractive enough, indeed, to cause the Admiralty to station naval vessels here at the time of the Napoleonic wars to support the customs service. Appledore's very own man-o'-war was the *Weazle*. Arriving here in the final years of the 18th century, she was a popular visitor, and local legend has it that there was an on-board frolic the night before she set sail on a Sunday morning in February 1799 to intercept a smuggling party bound for the secretive cove of Lee near Ilfracombe.

It was not a lucky voyage. Caught between Lundy and Baggy Point, she fired flares that could be seen and heard all round the helpless coast, but nobody could venture out against the gales that drove her on to the cliffs by Croyde. The first body ashore was that of a woman; perhaps the party had been too much for her and she had failed to go ashore on the previous night. Of the *Weazle* herself little remains, for all that could be salvaged was auctioned, but one of her cannon now guards the entrance to the Maritime Museum.

Smuggling, they say, was always a local pastime. In the old days, the tobacco came wrapped up inside furled sails, and even as I was putting together these sketches, local people were telling each other how the Customs men were stopping the ships as they came over the Bar after a police raid on an Appledore health club had turned up a few guns and apparently a lot of pornography. But, as the Ulster saying has it, "Mind you, I'm saying nothing."

~~~~~~~~~~

At one time where was a ferry here - a whole fleet of them, in fact, according to John Page who wrote a couple of guidebooks about Devon in the dying years of the

19th century. Writing of the beach at Crow, he describes how -

"We breathe once more, and walk onwards to the lighthouse - or lighthouses, for there are two - at the southern extremity of the three-mile long expanse. Between those lighthouses and Braunton, among the sandhills, less than a hundred years ago there stood the little chapel of St Ann, a building measuring only fourteen feet six inches by twelve.

To return to the lighthouses. They are both very ugly, and only one is of any height. The smaller is, indeed, a mere box mounted on a tramroad, on which it is moved to and fro according as the bar shifts it position. For the two lighthouses must be brought into one by vessels making for the estuary.

By walking along the beach to a point near the hospital ship at the back of the lighthouse we may signal for a boat to take us across to Instow. Probably it is some time before the fluttering handkerchief is noticed, but when it is, the boatmen will come fast enough, for a passage from the lighthouse means more pay than that from Instow to Appledore. As we are rowed across we get a still more extensive view of the "Barnstaple river" (as the people call the Taw), and on approaching Instow, the wooded slopes of Tapeley Park open out, crowned by the obelisk erected to the memory of Cornet Cleveland, who fell at Inkerman. Presently the keel grates on Instow Beach, and we pass up over the smooth, firm sands to the narrow fringe of villas that make up the more fashionable part of Instow.

Taking one of the ferry boats that lie waiting on the beach we cross to Appledore. As the boat draws near the end of our short voyage of half a mile or so we notice something of stir and bustle. Appledore, indeed, for so small a place, has a fair shipbuilding and ship-repairing trade, and dry dock accommodation for vessels of considerable burthen. Craft in all stages of repair and disrepair, and almost of every build, lie along the quay, or are moored up the river, and the sound of mallet and hammer comes merrily across the flood."

If those Victorian ferrymen took some time to respond to the fluttering handkerchiefs, they are hardly to be blamed if a local legend is to be trusted. And if you can't trust legends, where has the colour gone from life?

It seems that while some Appledore boatmen sat on Western Hill one quiet evening, a voice was heard calling from the lighthouse. Someone went to their boat and rowed across, thinking the caller needed to be ferried back to Appledore. The boat grounded on the gravel as the stranger approached, and he was told to climb aboard. As he did, though, the boatman's mate noticed something odd about the stranger. "My God, it's the devil!" he shouted, "Shove off!"

With a mighty heave, the boatman pushed his boat full astern back into the river. As the stranger had put his leg up over the gunwale of the boat, the mate had noticed that instead of a foot, the character had a cloven hoof.

Today, the ferry only runs to Crow if you book the trip in advance even if the ownership of the Appledore run has passed to our side of the river, but the beach over there at Crow Point is still an attractive local outing for any family who have access to a boat, or a friendly boatman, who can land them there between tides while the skipper gets on with the serious business of fishing over the bar. Be sure to choose a fisherman who is as skilful as he is friendly, for Crow is a tricky place to land, even more so when the tide is flooding, as the boat can be driven ashore and prove difficult to float off again.

The lighthouses are not what they were - "ugly" said Page of the Crow pair - "I would disagree," says local artist Tom Andrews about the Instow pair that now do their work, "the high one has beautiful timber shutters, and of course has a house with a lovely cobbled yard and several outbuildings. The actual lamp was, as I recall, a gas cylinder, but electrically timed. I remember visiting the light house as a boy. Incidentally, there was a large suspended ball on a nearby gantry which would be raised or lowered at half-tide. Also the gale warning cones would be hoisted there. Of course, the light house was manned in those days."

~~~~~~~~~~~~

Beyond the slip and the little beach you will see a cluster of industrial buildings. This is the yard where Alan Hinks has made fine wooden boats the way his father and grandfather did for a century and more; though not always on this site, for a Victorian entrepreneur (whose daughter still lives in the village) built a gasworks here. The directories of the day go into immense detail in describing the financing of the venture and the cost to its users of the 65 public lamps. Progress is not always in a forward direction, and great publicity was given in the 1970s to a move which put the cabling for the electric street lighting underground. If only we had stuck to gas, the overhead cables would never have been there in the first place. Come to that, the cables still snake all over (or rather above) the road which gives the visitor his first impression of the village. Progress doesn't always manage to reach the end of the journey.

TURNING TO EBB

Next shift at the shipyards

The tide is turning now, for the river, and for the men who make ships on it. Here in the heart of the village is the one-time Richmond Dry Dock, empty and derelict now behind its blind walls, its two giant cranes still carrying a visual reminder to every visitor that Appledore once owed more to industry than it does now to tourism. One day, we may be a Mousehole or a Mevagissey; one day, but not yet.

Upstream stands out - in every sense of the word - the great hanger of the Bidna Yard, largest covered yard of its kind in Europe when it was built in 1970. Bidna has passed through a flotilla of owners in its short and unsettled life, from local ownership to nationalisation and back to a private owner once more. In the last few months of its life in the British Shipbuilders' empire, "Appledore Ferguson" provided a brief stay of execution for welders from the doomed North Eastern Shipbuilders yard at Sunderland.

The men who work at Bidna practise some of the highest skills in Devon; skills of computer-aided design with full-colour screens that can show you every angle of a ship, inside and out, at a touch on a keyboard, but also, of course, the traditional skills of bending and cutting steel into the subtle curves of a dredger or a ferry. Car-makers may think they do the same sort of work, but they don't work with plates of sheet steel half an inch thick and thirty feet long. Electricians and laggers work buried in tropical temperatures inside the hull while the throbbing and hammering of the shipwrights goes on around them.

It's all a far cry from Westacott's old yard at Churchfield by the Seagate Hotel -

> "Here, beside the offices of the firm, are the blacksmith's shop and the boat-builders, sailmakers' and blockmakers' lofts. Under the sail-loft are sawpits, the circular saw with its manifold advantages having been introduced in this department of the business."

Then, when Westacotts moved to the New Quay in 1881, they brought fine new machinery from Glasgow and Yorkshire including the Bear punching machine -

> "by the concentration of great pressure in a single screw, it enables a hole to be cut by one man through iron three fourths of an inch thick with the greatest ease, what was formerly the work of twenty minutes being thus accomplished in two."

Technological advances were no less dramatic in 1889 than they are today.

~~~~~~~~~~

But there have been - and there still are - other shipbuilders in Appledore. At the opposite end of the village, on the road to the Burrows, Alan Hinks maintains the traditional ways and builds in wood. High-prowed fishing boats would take shape in a lofty shed with the air of a mediaeval cathedral or a tithe barn, utterly in tone with the great replica galleons that were launched from here.

The *Nonsuch* was launched from here in 1968, stood up to the worst of the Cornish Atlantic gales en route to Falmouth, but was ignominiously shipped across the Atlantic to the Canadian Lakes and the Man and Life

Museum in Winnipeg. Four years later the *Golden Hinde* made it under her own sails through the Panama Canal to a triumphant landfall in San Francisco. Commanding the seas as confidently as Drake's original, the *Hinde* sailed on to Japan and back to England, circling the world before crossing the Atlantic once more and coasting - if the word is not too cheap - between the Caribbean and Canada.

Between the two working yards is the shell of the Richmond Yard, where one of the earliest patent slips was built in Devon. Its great cranes still hover above the riverside scene; curiously at home among the gentle Torridge-side hills, they feature in several paintings by the late Peter Reid alongside the more obvious attractions of the Quay or Silver Street.

The Richmond Dock was the creation of William Yeo, who opened it in 1856 to refit and repair the ships trading between Appledore and his father's business in Prince Edward Island. The transatlantic trade enriched the Yeo family as much as it brought work to Appledore. In the museum at Charlottetown in Prince Edward Island, you may see the advertisement soliciting passengers for the maiden Atlantic crossing of the *Ocean Queen* to present themselves to Mr William Yeo in that town or to James Beara in Appledore, England.

Richmond House still lords it over the entrance to the village, even if its rooms have been turned into flats, and its name changed to "The Holt". Older Appledore folk still call Richmond Road "Dark Lane" in memory of the Canadian oaks which once overshadowed the old and narrow way down to the creek.

That word "creek" suggests just how much this part of Appledore has changed; indeed there have been more changes here than any other part of the village, yet in typical Appledore style, the turn-of-the-century postcard views are still recognisable as the foundation for today. The earliest river frontage followed the curving line of the "drang" which runs off Marine Parade next to the

23

butcher's shop, round by Silver Street and on towards the main quay.

The new dock reclaimed land opposite Marine Parade and the old Narrow Quay, and stone walls closed the river off from view. Then the drive down to the new Richmond Dock was widened and developed, and finally the remaining island of old cottages close to the fire station was cleared and a brave new road driven through from the point at the top of the hill where the old road into Appledore went on over Staddon and down to the church.

The Dock and the village depended on the Yeos more than they knew, and when William Yeo died in 1872, the trade collapsed. A hungry ten years went by before Robert Cock moved his business to the Richmond Dock from Churchfield. "Appledore has a future before it", declared a writer on North Devon's industries in a book published only a few years after the move. Ship-repairing, he said, was "now limited only by the restricted accommodation" and "once the loadstone of capital is applied to the enterprise which awaits its attractive metal, the prosperity and the growth of Appledore will be assured." The arguments over the sale of Bidna to a private developer still turn on how much of the loadstone is needed to make British ship-building competitive. Some things here never change.

At much the same time as Robert Cock leased Richmond, Westacotts took over the neighbouring New Quay, only to wait months on end before the first order arrived. When it did, the excitement was enough for a Westacott shipwright to burst into the church during Sunday service and shout out that "the barque is over the bar!" A century on, and the future of Bidna - whoever owns it - always seems to hang in exactly the same way on the next order being confirmed before the work on the present one has finished.

~~~~~~~~~

Richmond Dock had one final burst of activity, when a new breed of shipwrights came here to build the most curious vessels that were ever floated through the massive old gates. The new bridge that sweeps so high over the Torridge two miles to the south of Appledore stands on piers of concrete, two of which began their life here as "650 tonne cellular caisson starter bases." In layman's terms, these were huge, hollow steel and concrete boxes, neatly built inside the old dock before being floated out and tugged upstream to be lowered into position,but 650 tonnes of steel and concrete is about the size of a bungalow and just about as manoeuvrable.

When the word went round (as it does on these occasions) that the first caisson was to be taken upstream, half the village turned out (as they do on these occasions) in the driving sleet of a February night in 1985; the caisson had been inched out on the high spring tide early that morning, clearing the dock sill with only 6" to spare underneath, and only a couple of feet clearance on either side of the dock gate, filled with compressed air to lift it out, and guided by a tug to wait in the parlour for the evening tide. Floodlights and hard hats seemed to be everywhere as the lumbering juggernaut lurched slowly into the deep water channel and headed into the darkness.

Every time a new Appledore ship sails out across the bar, she is waved and cheered off by crowds along the Quay, with as many handkerchiefs wiping away surreptitious tears as waving to the sea trials crew. But this was different; this could hardly be called a ship, and she, if she were a "she", was heading away from the sea, not towards it, and the mood that drew the crowds was one more of curiosity than maritime pride.

When the second caisson, locally called a "gazzoon", left Appledore a month later, only a handful watched her maiden voyage. Still, better for the old dock to have ended its career in such a unique way than to have simply rotted away.

25

Today, the Richmond Dock is a shell, sold off to a local consortium (why does that word always sound as if it has something to hide ?) who sold it on to developers who plan in their turn to develop it as a riverside residential site - "yuppie flats", say the locals, while the conservationists wonder what will happen to the historical hole in the ground that was once a marvel of modern marine engineering.

~~~~~~~~~~

Nothing is ever quite straight in Appledore. That's only right in a place where they build ships, and perhaps the new estates on your right and left as you turn the corner and begin to come down the hill into the village don't quite look right because their lines are too straight. The roads curve as they follow the river bank, or as they track alongside the one-time streams that fed the river. The houses curve: upwards from the broad bases that are essential when building with cob or pebbles, but horizontally, too, as they follow the roads, and the best Appledore houses curve in both directions at once as much as any inland Devon cottage. Tradition says that ships' timbers are the reason; my guess is that shipwrights who worked on improving their homes carried home with them the skills and design principles of the shipyard.

Straight lines are out of place here. When a neighbour of mine fitted a nameplate to his house, he tried to place it correctly with a spirit-level. It seemed to climb uphill against the lines of the road. He set it parallel to the doorway. It sat askew from the window. He measured the distance to align it with the window. It made the doorway look aslant. Eventually, he did what Appledore home-owners must have done for centuries. He held the nameplate against the wall and slid it around until it looked right. Then he drilled the holes and screwed it to the brickwork. It's a little bit out of line of with everything; but, somehow, it fits.

26

In the same manner, the track which followed the other side of the creek here curves uphill away from the water's edge and over the bluff to the flatter land around Bidna Farm. Then the development consortia of their day - headed by the ubquitous and ingenious Thomas Benson - built a new quay south of the creek, and drove a road alongside it, which they naturally called New Quay Street.

Few parts of Appledore are as well concealed as this road. So narrow is it that cars can pass only at well-chosen places and even then with the breath held in; so narrow that the brewers' deliveries to the Bell Inn close the road completely. Yet alongside this narrow lane, hemmed in one side by a clifflike hillside wall and on the other by the river, are houses which merit the estate agent's clichéd "sought after".

One of the features that those estate agents never fail to highlight when they have one of our properties on their books is the four-sided glass loft that looks so much like a greenhouse or conservatory perched precariously at the highest point of the roof. Today they are for lounging, but their original purpose was to allow the village merchant a chance to save money: looking out from the loft when his vessel was expected, the owner could postpone hiring stevedores until the moment she crossed the bar.

Above the one-time quarry along this road was once the logical development of that arrangement: Chanter's Folly was a three-storey tower raised at the one point where a watchman could see out to Hartland and his signals could be seen on Bideford Quay.

"Chanter" after the Bideford shipowner who built it, and "Folly" because it was said that Mr Chanter only found out too late that it didn't work; only when he climbed to its top storey did he discover that he couldn't see over Northam's ridge to the open sea by Hartland Point. That's one version of the story, but Vernon Boyle calls in local witnesses to dispute what may have been a vain attempt by Appledore folk to belittle their upstream rivals. He also suggests in a non-committal way that the name "Folly" arose from the legend that the first ship to be seen from the tower was commanded by Chanter's son, and "the old man saw her wrecked with the loss of all hands before she could take the Bar."

A quiet road this, with glimpses of the sea between the walls of the yards, but watch out for the passing juggernaut once you have passed the site of Chanter's Folly. Any decline in water-borne traffic in and out of Appledore has been more than balanced by the arrival of larger and larger road vessels whose home ports are scattered around the village, yet among the many perplexing actions of the people who build roads in North Devon has been the decision to alter the alignment of the junction where our road joins the new Northam by-pass, so that the massive hulks bound for Bidna, the quayside warehouses along this narrow road, or any one of the local haulage firms bring traffic to a halt as they manoeuvre their way round the "improved" layout.

~~~~~~~~~~~~

Above and beyond the Bidna yard is Knapp House, where lived that Thomas Benson whom I mentioned just now. A merchant in tobacco and fish, he won a government contract to transport convicts to Maryland; a resourceful entrepreneur, he took out a lease on Lundy Island and staffed it with convict labour - "he often said that the sending of convicts to Lundy was the same as sending them to America; they were transported from England, it matters not where so long as they were out of the country."

That was in 1748, and it lost him the contract. Another moneyspinner was called for, and in 1752, he conceived the idea of chartering a vessel, loading it with valuable cargo, insuring both heavily and taking his profit by

28

contriving to "lose" both vessel and cargo conveniently close to Lundy and claiming the insurance.

He selected a Captain Lancey of Northam for the command, and hired Thomas Powe, an Appledore tailor of ill reputation, to recruit the rest of the crew. The chosen vessel was the *Nightingale*, and she was (somewhat sketchily) fitted out at Boathyde, the riverside house beyond the Bidna yard.

Off Lundy, the crew were put in the picture and their silence bought in the time-honoured way. The cargo was off-loaded, the poor *Nightingale* was holed, and a fire set, and the blame laid on the unhappy Lundy convicts. A passing ship rescued them, tried unsuccessfully to land them in South Wales and returned them, ominously, to Knapp House.

Sensing the need for a rescue operation, Benson drilled Captain Lancey in what he should report to the inevitable enquiry, and took him off to his lawyer in Bideford. In the meantime, the bosun who had been recruited by Powe, one James Bather, was drinking his way round Barnstaple with his version of events and gathering up the courage to ask Benson for a bigger share of silence money.

Rather unjustly, it was Lancey who was arrested, rather than Bather or Benson, and he was soon on his way to London for trial, followed by other members of the crew. Benson offered bail with the clear intention of shipping them all out of the country, but his kindly offer was declined, not least because enquiries were under way into his tobacco dealings, helped along by some of his rival merchants. A tactical retreat to Portugal seemed prudent.

Lancey, Powe and the others remained to face their judges. In due course, Lancey faced his Maker at Wapping, Powe was remanded until 1758, and the others were released. The prime mover of it all kept on the move, one step ahead of extradition until his death nearly twenty years later.

Benson left his mark on Appledore in more ways than one – he built the New Quay Dock, he furnished firm evidence for all the scurrilous tales that outsiders love to tell about Appledore seamen, and he was linked by marriage to the Melhuish family – but you will have to wait until you reach Bude Street to find out the significance of that particular matter.

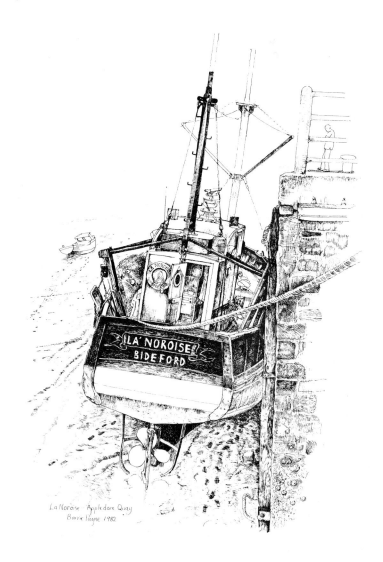

La Noroise Appledore Quay
Barry Payne 1982

HALF-EBB

Mid-morning in Market St.

Market Street is what it says it is. Here was the village market on the Quay, now a café with a fish-and-chip shop lurking behind it. It opened as a pannier market in 1844; "pannier" because it was the sort of market to which people brought their produce in panniers, to be distinguished from cattle markets and stock markets.

A shame that it went. A smaller version of the markets that survive in places like Barnstaple, Bideford and Bridgwater, it mixed the weekly stall-holders' tables with the up-market traders who could afford little lock-up shops. In the days when you bought unwrapped goods from real people in a building like this, shared as it was with a coal merchant's cellar and the Boy Scouts' Hall, shopping had a human dimension that no amount of musical wallpaper and bar-coded checkouts can ever replace.

Yet in Market Street still are the shops where all of the village needs (or, to be honest, most of them) can usually be met. You might have to drive into Bideford for the plastic wrapped goods of the supermarket, for petrol, or the comically misnamed "consumer durables", but the shops here will supply you with fresh bread and groceries, and the butchers will do something which no supermarket anywhere has done for a very long time, that is let you choose your own joints and cuts off the carcase.

Some of the Appledore shops look as if they try to cater for the self-service taste, but somehow it doesn't quite come off. The gondolas, the chilled food cabinets and the checkouts are there, but it's rather like someone speaking

31

a foreign language; however fluently it's done, you can tell it's not a native accomplishment and that the speaker would be happier using the tongue he was born with.

The butcher in Market Street is a real butcher - certificates to prove it, a colour photo of his shop window overflowing with one-time bulls, sheep and pigs that won market prizes and still carry their rosettes into the after-life; and hanging behind the counter are their distant relations. Not a shrink-wrapped and pre-weighed package in sight, and pride of place in the window display goes to the locally made "Appledore sausage."

A comparative newcomer to the village, this butcher has gingerly begun to try out his sense of humour on the locals; when some scaffolding went up across the road from his shop, one side of the billboard that normally advertises his wares told us to watch out for the multi-storey car park, and the other advised us that this was the start of a precinct for which Marks & Spencers and Sainsburys had already reserved units. His next billboard warned us all "three weeks to Christmas, order your Easter eggs now." Watch this space.

Across the road until recently stood the Appledore Studio, an art gallery and the ideal neighbour for a butcher if you are going to put shops into a small village. No doubt the planners would have found it neater to put all the food shops in one precinct and the art galleries in another; but places like Appledore developed centuries ago without the help - and maybe in spite of the help - of the planners of such things. And just as well, too. We do our best to keep up those old customs.

Wander down the road a little, past the chandlery and past "Cobwebs" the home of unconsidered trifles, established in a little shop that was once a fishmonger and before then a sweet shop; and the same happy mix of shops crops up again. On the one side, a grocer advises you, with justice, that if you want to eat real home-cooked ham and not the plastic variety, he has it on offer.   True, but he makes curiously little of the selection of dried fruit which people drive across Devon to buy.

Across the road from Boyle's stores, the jeweller's shop cheerfully mixes souvenirs and video hire with antique jewellery and expert watch and clock repair.   If the jeweller himself isn't in, he may be in Bideford or in France; or he may just as likely be out on Lundy repairing the church clock.

Led on by the smell of fresh bread from the corner café and bakery,   you pass a window display for yet another art gallery.   If you were to walk on to the end of Market Street, you would come to the Appledore Pine Shop: and to a sign in its window directing you back the way you came to its new home amid an Aladdin's cave of curtains, bedspreads and all kinds of lace at the bottom of Bude Street.   If you obeyed that sign, you would then come across the signs for the Gallery in One End Street and the new Appledore Gallery further up Bude Street.

Perhaps the most curious shop of all was the one that has now gone: in one window were flowers, fruit and vegetables in harmonious mixture; in the other were bread, sticky buns, iced cakes and fancies, while the back of the shop was piled high with knitting wool and patterns.   On the pavement outside, according to season, were trays of bedding plants or vegetables, flowering shrubs and cut flowers, or sacks of potatoes. It opened when the owner arrived in an estate car with the day's wares, and closed when most of them had been sold. Like so much else in Appledore, it had the happy sense of being something more than a hobby and something less than a merely boring business.

Yet, however busy it all seems now, the commercial life of the village is only a shadow of what it was a little over fifty years ago, as the directories of the day vividly illustrate.   Notice, will you,   that in those benighted pre-war days,   there was a chemist (and a doctor) right here on the Quay - no expensive bus trips to a Health Centre in Northam or a chemist in Bideford. All those people working on ships, their cargoes, their fittings like pulley blocks or sails, or the oilskins made by Mr Beara - that is clear enough, but it is a little hard to believe that Appledore could sustain no fewer than two dozen hotels and guest houses in the days before mass tourism invented the Golden Coast and the Tarka country trail.

~~~~~~~~~~

Appledore today is full of artists and craftsmen: like the shops, they prefer the old, more personal, way. Most of them work for pleasure and their own satisfaction first, and earn a crust or two as an afterthought. That's not to say that their work is not worth buying; some of it is excellent, and at a price well below comparable work in places like St Ives that think they have a reputation to preserve.

Some of them only take a little finding. You can buy local work in the galleries in Market Street or Irsha Street; further up Irsha Street, you can buy wool and knitwear handspun in the tiny front room of "Charlie of Appledore", or if you walk up One End Street or Bude Street, Barrie Payne and Gerard Lindley will sell you their own work, just as Stuart Rogers sells his woodcarvings from his house on Marine Parade.

The others hide their lights under a collection of bushels. Elderly ladies (and a few younger ones) still make the unique Appledore sweaters or "frocks", knitted from fine worsted wool as if they were socks or gloves, with a handful of small needles. Waterproof and windproof, the Appledore frock has a unique design across the shoulders to protect the owner's shoulders when carrying oars or heaving ropes while alive - and, it is said, to help to identify his body if the sea claims his life. The design is unique to Appledore, and local knitters will tell you that the handiwork of each knitter is as clear as a signature.

There are, as well, a few fishermen who still make Appledore mats of sennit that will outlast any mass-produced doormat of coir and look better into the bargain. There is a lady who models in clay but doesn't say too much about the days when she fashioned gold and silver in Hatton Garden. A corner room just off the Quay houses a litho press sought out by fine artists from miles away. There are people who make fine work from clay or fine toys and games from wood and people whose embroidery is in a quite different league from the conventional work of cross stitch kits. A glance through a few windows hints at people who paint — and buy — pictures of considerable quality.

In the kitchen of the Maritime Museum, a ring-backed binder celebrates the many crafts workers of the village in a typically low-key way. Those photographs somehow symbolise the way Appledore folk live with their artists: they enjoy their work, they even admire it, and perhaps sometimes they are proud of it — but these artists and craftsmen are the friends and neighbours they meet in the shops and the pubs of the village. After all, they are just people living alongside other people who have traditionally followed equally challenging crafts and professions building ships and sailing them on the high seas. Let us always keep a sense of proportion in all things.

LOW WATER

Lunch by the Church

The tide is right out now, and the sands are exposed all
the way to Instow. Don't let the narrow channel fool
you: every so often the bolder-than-average boy tries to
walk across, believing that a strip of water only forty
or fifty feet across has to be shallow. Maybe it is at
spring tide, but the current does not make it fordable,
and outside spring tides the channel is still deep enough
to put the boldest boy out of his depth. One pair who
tried crossing the river from Instow to the pool here a
couple of years ago were picked up by the inshore
lifeboat half way to the Bar in the few seconds it took
for the boat to be launched once the alarm was raised.

Here is the boundary between Appledore and West
Appledore. "Boundary" is not too strong a word. The
pub here is the Seagate, and when you look along the
Quay, especially from the water, it really does look like
a sea-wall defence, and the break here would be the
natural gateway to the village from the sea - the
natural sea-gate.

A century ago, this was also the main gateway to the
village. A ferry once ran here from the Great Field of
Braunton, and if it ran today, it would still save you an
hour's frustration in the sluggish train of traffic that
runs through Barnstaple to bring you to that other bank,
less than a mile away across the river. A century ago,
you could walk to the end of the old quay, stroll down
the slip towards a little beach, and cross it to the
patent slip by Cock's Churchfield Yard, climbing up again
to the other half of Appledore. A century ago, if you
wanted to visit West Appledore, that was the only way to
Irsha Street from here.

I suppose you might call this area the heart of the village. If you have the energy, you can play on the swings and roundabouts of the tiny playground, or if you are too big, too grown-up and too self-conscious, it's almost as much fun to watch the children.

This little no-man's land between the two villages was the battleground of many a junior test match in the school holidays in the days before video, skateboards and the BMX machine. The wickets were always "crickets" (small wooden stools stood on end) provided by some unbeknowing mum. One wonders whether the name for the stool arose from that clandestine usage, or if it occurred to some young lateral thinker that something called a cricket had to have a role in the game.

Sheltered suntrap in the summer, this corner can catch the wind in the winter. Puzzled beach-walkers on Instow sands one winter eventually identified the 20-foot wide plastic orange saucer that had arrived unannounced on their beach as the lid of the slide from our playground, lifted off its mountings and bounced from wave to wave across the choppy estuary. Mind you, the same storm snapped the mooring cables of the Appledore lifeboat and left her aground on Crow Point.

But you can put that sort of thought to the back of your mind if you are sitting outside the Seagate with a pint in your hand and a bar snack on the table in front of you. Come back in the evening, and the setting will be just as fine, and you'll be able to listen to the town band as well as watch the passing scene. But now, in the middle of the day, with the water at its lowest, the highest excitement of the day will be the echoes of the paddlers and their dogs in the maze of toddler-sized pools on Instow beach.

There is no longer a beach on this side of the river; it was originally replaced by a tide-washed swimming pool which, after its annual clean, would within a fortnight start filling up with general detritus as well as many unwanted and sometimes unspeakable items generously, if surreptitiously, donated by their diffident owners.

That pool gave way, in its turn to a beachcomber's corner below the sea wall by the playground which was built in order to link the two halves of the village, but the magnetic attraction of the corner for unconsidered trifles is as powerful as ever. Bricks worn as smooth as pebbles were the most common find, but elegant lumps of elderly gas cookers, curiously mis-shapen bicycles, and driftwood were there for the taking. And now, a vast apron for touring cars has been stretched out from the Quay to the Point, turning a gentle curving beach into a hard grey desert. As I keep saying, progress isn't always a blessing, and the compulsion to keep everything in its place sits ill on disorderly old villages.

~~~~~~~~~~

There is only one sign of honest toil visible from here at this stage of the tide, and that's decently far off, over at Crow Point. The gravel barges lie there as they have done for decades; only the techniques have changed with the years. The principle remains the same - ground the empty barge at mid-tide on the beach, fill it with coarse sand and gravel to the very limit of its hold, then wait until the tide floats it off. Then you can drive it slowly back across the river to Appledore, where you off-load the gravel in to trucks that will take it away to become part of anything from a smart garden patio to a a suburban road system. Meanwhile, the eternal action of the sea will roll massive boulders around Hartland Point until they become smaller boulders at Bucks Mills, pebbles on the ridge at Westward Ho! and finally sand and gravel at Crow, ready for the next barge.

Only the technique has changed. Today a little yellow JCB lifts the sodden loads on to the barge. Time was, when men with shovels had to fling the stuff, like tossing bales of straw, several feet above their heads and over the gunwales into the holds of the barges.

The most exciting - and apprehensive - time was when the laden barges "fleeted off". Gunwale deep, no freeboard, and a quickly flowing tide; a dead weight sluggishly reluctant to move, like some awakening leviathan - then off, and in with the tide.

One local bargee, Georgie Schiller, was believed to have been knocked off his barge by a swinging tiller. Like most local seamen, he was unable to swim, and drowned in sight of his destination and his home.

How satisfying to sit with that pint in your hand and hear only the barking and the laughter and the distant chugging of the engines over at Crow. Turn your back on the modern cars, and the electronic gadgetry of the pub, forget what you paid for your pint, and you could be back in that holiday era, somewhere in the 30s or the 50s when the sun always shone for the annual fortnight down in glorious Devon. And you have caught a little of the special attraction of Appledore.

~~~~~~~~~~

The Seagate may be the central pub in the village. It's not the only one: in the quayside middle of Appledore, there are three others, along Irsha Street a further two, and one more on the way to the Bidna Yard. All of them different, all of them with their special clientele. And all of them a fraction of the pubs that once crowded the village streets. The 1856 directory lists all seven of the pubs that remain, plus the *Full Moon*, the *Globe*, the *Red Lion*, the *Ship*, the *Unicorn*, the *Swan*, the *Crown and Sceptre*, the *Mariners' Arms*, and the *Shipwrights' Arms*. Thirsty work, the fishing.

There was once - and how welcome it must have been among all those excuses for refreshment - a gents' urinal across the quay to your right. Usefully combining the needs of nature with the skills of the sea, it was said that if you stood by the flagpole next to the urinal and faced the old light-house, you were pointing due north.

Across to your left as you sit in front of the Grand Hotel (as the Seagate was once known), the jutting point of land was once a modern slipway and shipbuilders' yard, but times have moved on, and hardly anyone remembers the place as Gribble's Point, though the older folk may still talk of such things to each other.

The other landmark in this quarter is, of course, the parish church. Built - and "prettily embowered", according to the 1878 directory - on the site of the ancient chapel of St Anne (or, as less romantic historians claim, on the ruins of a cowshed), it was dedicated to St Mary in 1838 after a four-year campaign by the Appledore residents of Northam parish, who complained about having to bury their dead a couple of miles away in the Northam graveyard. Two miles is something of a trek when you have to carry the coffin, and something of an injustice when your community outnumbers the mother parish. At any rate, 600 of the flock raised over £1000 towards the cost of their own church; a near-run thing, as the accounts show a credit balance of only £3.0s.2d once all bills were met.

If Appledore folk drank hard, they also took their religion seriously, as everyone does who lives in close quarters with the sea, and this tiny community still supports the three Free Church congregations that they raised money to build at much the same time as St Mary's was dedicated. The Seamen's Mission has shrunk to a fraction of its original size, though, and the schools that they built with their churches have passed on to other purposes.

Yet those independent congregations also once had to make pilgrimage every Sunday to the godly parish of Northam. It strikes one as a little odd that a village with such a proud and ancient tradition of seafaring and ship-building should not have a place of worship that dates back earlier than the middle of the 19th century. Even the Cistercians only built a lodging house, not a chapel. Maybe that's why our more pious neighbours say we used to eat missionaries. Maybe we did eat missionaries. Or maybe it's only that rich harvest of alehouses.

It might even be just a little touch of jealousy: a decade or more ago, Bideford had her Bucanneers, Torrington her Cavaliers, and Appledore her Pirates - nothing sinister or pseudo-historical, merely groups of high-spirited and well-minded folk who had a lot of fun (and gave a lot of fun) raising money for local good causes. Alongside the more genteel charity of the Rotary or the Round Table, the Buccanneers, the Cavaliers and the Pirates had a brashness and inventiveness all their own; the Cavaliers even made the Guinness Book of Records for their mammoth annual bonfires. But they burnt themselves out, and then the Buccanneers gave up their freebooting exploits - only the Appledore Pirates remain, annually raising money so that their elderly neighbours might have a more joyful Christmas.

~~~~~~~~~~

Standing high above the church is the Edwardian vicarage, latest in a series of clergy houses which have grown progressively smaller and less picturesque over the years. The one which the locals still call "the vicarage" passed into private hands a few years ago, and more recently became an old folks' home.

But before its new role in life, the old vicarage played host to many a clerical character. Nothing in the Parson Jack Russell breed, perhaps, but the Revd Hugh Christian Andreas Sigvold ("Yewcas" for short) Muller was a figure of legend if ever there was one.

Not only did he turn a blind eye to the inevitable furtive cigarette puffed after Bible Class; he presented a Woodbine to every member at the annual Christmas party. When he travelled to Northam on "The Pride of the West", as one of the local coaches was ambitiously named, it was not enough to offer his seat to a lady - the Vicar offered his lap, and on one occasion when a hard bulge clearly disconcerted one such passenger, he promptly explained that "it's not what you think it is, my dear, it's only my pen and a bottle of ink."

A Naval chaplain in the first World War, a member of the lifeboat crew, and a passionate devotee of the local football league, he was in every sense the father-in-God to the parish of Appledore for over fifty years, and when he died, they stood in silence at the Bideford ground before the Barnstaple Derby match.

More recently, the souls of the village were in the capable hands of the colourful Donald Peyton Jones, who did his rounds on horseback and persuaded his Lundy Island parishioners to treat Wednesday as Sunday so that he could take services there midweek instead of at the weekend. He kept up the Lundy connection long after leaving Appledore for South Devon, explaining that the official pastor suffered from seasickness, and remarking after one visit that he had given them "enough services to see them through until I call back in six weeks' time."

His successor kept rabbits. To be pedantic, he usually kept them, but every so often lost them, which was, I suppose, one way to meet his parishioners, at least those among his parishioners who found the huge lop-eared beasts munching their way through vegetable plots, flower border and even shrubberies.

And now the village has a vicar who has campaigned for the homeless by sleeping for a midwinter month or so in a cardboard box outside his church in South Devon and had the organist play "Blaydon Races" as a voluntary when one of the Sunderland welders married a local maid. If nothing else, the established church keeps us well entertained.

43

YOUNG FLOOD

Afternoon in Bude Street and Odun Road

The tide may have begun to turn, but there is still not enough water to return the river to work. Time to head inland.

Bude Street tries to be straight, but doesn't quite make it. Halfway up the hill, for no very obvious reason, it flicks a little to the right, but remembers its dignity, and goes back again to the straight and fairly narrow. There are no yellow lines here, because Murphy's Law applies to all who park cars outside their house; the street that has been silent and empty for hours before you stopped to unload the week's groceries suddenly turns into a small-scale rush hour. It's even worse if you want to paint your house: the first car can be guaranteed to turn into Bude Street not when you start climbing, but the moment your foot touches the top rung of the ladder.

It's a dignified sort of place, but dignified in the way that people in a dentist's crowded waiting room, sitting bunched together among the elderly magazines, are dignified. All housing life is here. Four-square Victorian brick villas sit close by cob cottages of an earlier day; one of the High Street banks clung to its business by its twice-weekly finger nails until the spring of 1990, but only the name remains of the other one further up the hill, and you wouldn't know from a casual glance that a pair of cottages at the top of Bude Street were once the local nick, complete with cells (though a descendant of the man who built them will tell you that they were originally malthouses), and a couple of local bobbies.

45

One or two of the houses pull their skirts delicately back from the pavement, but most of them sit it out brazenly, their owners doing the decent thing and leaving the curtains pulled back in the evenings, so that the passing flow of tourists can look in and admire the antiques and the floppy easy chairs. Some of those front parlours may look more cramped than cosy, but all Bude Street houses, especially those on the left as you walk up the hill, have hidden depths - literally. The gardens here go back for a hundred yards or more, and many of those tiny little cottages run to four or five bedrooms, some of them tucked into attics with windows that look out over the scree of pitched roofs all the way down to the river's edge.

Many of the Bude Street homes, however, carry an invisible time bomb. See an estate agent's sign, view the house, and put in an offer. Sooner or later (usually later), your solicitor will gently break the news to you that you are the prospective owner of a "Melhuish house." What that means is that someone, somewhere, *might* turn out to be the freeholder of the land on which your house is built.

Squire Melhuish was an 18th century landowner with money problems. He sold off parcels of land on 200-year leases, but regrettably omitted to make sure that his descendants were around to claim back the land when the leases came to an end in 1970. For a time, panic reigned, then the insurance companies came to the rescue, and you will need to add a little consideration to the purchase price of your house, just to make sure that a long-lost Melhuish cousin doesn't crawl out of the woodwork to claim your back garden as his, and start charging you a suitably inflated ground rent. It hasn't happened so far, but all the local lawyers will tell you that it's better to play safe. Well, they would, wouldn't they ? Especially as nobody ever seems to have paid any ground rent in the days of those putative leases.

Odun Road is where old Appledore ended; beyond the sweep of houses overlooking the river there was once

46

only farmland. And 'once' was not too long ago - when Devon County Council published its conservation study of Appledore in the early 1970s, the maps it used showed not a single house other than The Holt up the hill from Odun Road.

There are people who can remember coming to the one-time Odun Farm for eggs, milk or cream after the evening milking. You can still buy eggs there, but the dairy, its horse and cart, churns and jugs went years ago, even if the local folk still talk of calling in at "the farm shop" for free-range eggs from Hamish's seraglio.

That's not to say that Appledore has lost its dairies: rival rounds make the daily drops, and one of them is the famous Hocking's Dairy whose luscious ice-cream is a tourist attraction in its own right, carrying in every lick the flavour of the ideal (and probably pre-war) Devon holiday.

~~~~~~~~~~

A century ago, the heights above Appledore were farmed from Bude House, sitting at the top of Bude Street with the farm manager's house on one side and its outbuildings on the other. The manager's house became Odun Farm and took over the last of the old farm, while the outbuildings were imaginatively converted into half a dozen houses in the 1970s.

Two other houses stood high above the village: Staddon House was the first vicarage for Appledore; since then, successive vicarages have slipped downhill. The middle one, built in 1901 and now known as the "old" vicarage, was sold into private hands, and later became a residential home for elderly people who all, one hopes, sleep soundly in their beds untroubled by the ghosts who - well, leave it to the owner to explain :

"It was a Tuesday night in April, 1984. I watched the 10 o'clock news downstairs in the kitchen, made myself a cup of coffee and went to bed. As our bedroom was still being decorated I slept in the room we call the 'Blue and Orange Room', our principal guest bedroom. This was the only room in the house with bars on the windows, suggesting that children played there once.

The door was open and at 2.00am I awoke to hear the radio on, very loudly, in the kitchen. I knew I had not left it on, nor had the alarm on it been set. I waited a few minutes and then the radio went off. Even modern alarm radios don't go on and off by themselves - I was therefore convinced that there were intruders. Having a phone by my bed, I dialled 999 and explained the situation.

The Police arived promptly and searched the house. They found no one and no signs of entry. They re-assured me that this was all part of a night's work and that's what they are there for. On their way out of the house one of the policemen unplugged the radio.

I went upstairs to bed again at about 3.15am, feeling quite safe, and tried to get back to sleep. It was about 4.00am when I awoke with a buzzing sensation in my ears and I saw two little girls standing on the right of my bed. They stood there laughing at me as if to say, 'Silly girl, calling the Police, it was only us playing around.'

In the morning I recalled this experience vividly and immediately. The girls were aged about 7 and 9, both had blonde hair, one cut in a 'bob' style and the other

48

longer but neat. They were wearing Victorian style smock dressed with a little rounded lace collar. I mentioned this experience to a friend of mine in Appledore who said that she had seen a little girl playing 'Peek a Boo' when she used to help with the Parish Magazine.

The first time my stepson Richard came to the house, we were showing some local friends our garden. When we returned to the sitting room, Richard was pale and anxious. He asked whether there was ever a Rev. Miller or Muller. When we told him that the incumbent before the last two was called Rev. Muller he said that he had heard someone with a limp walking across the floor above (our bedroom) and heard a female voice say 'Good Morning, Rev. Muller'. As Richard had only just walked into the house, there was no way he could have had any knowledge of previous incumbents. We made local enquiries and discovered that the Revd Muller had a housekeeper – Miss Elmore, who had a pronounced limp, wore long black clothes and spent most of her life tending the graves in the churchyard."

Judy Chard includes that story in her "Tales of the Unexplained in Devon", and goes on to tell how she took a photo of the new owner in the Blue & Orange Room: the negative appeared blank, but it produced a normal contact print. A girlish trick, perhaps ? When asked for his comments, the last vicar to live in the haunted vicarage, remarked "Vicarages are a spiritual refuge, very homely and peaceful places. I could give them a whole list of people who still walk there."

That vicar was, of course, the Revd Donald Peyton Jones. I once asked him about the ghosts; "Dear me, yes. Of course there are ghosts there, there are always ghosts in vicarages. I tell everyone its the old vicars coming back to switch on the TV to keep up to date with what's going on down here. I told the good lady up the road just to go off to bed with her husband and have a good night's sleep and don't worry about any ghosts at all."

~~~~~~~~~~

"The Holt" was built as Richmond House by William Yeo, who was the founder of modern shipbuilding in Appledore. It was Yeo who built the Richmond Dock in 1853 and ran it until his death. His grand house went on the market in 1903, when it included The Mount as a "two-storey summerhouse with views" as well as stables and a farm. It has since been converted into flats, its grounds have become a rather tawdry public park and the priceless and beautiful trees brought here from all over the world have gone, substituted - in no sense replaced - by unimaginative houses more suited to a suburb than a working riverside village, while The Mount is now an estate of council houses enjoying the same views as the Yeos must have seen from their summer house.

Back in Odun Road, no scars remain of the stormy quarrel that led to the building of the pair of Edwardian cottages next to the car park. Legend has it that the owners of Odun Farm and Odun Villa fell out with each other at the turn of the century. Unable to resolve the dispute, the owners of Odun Villa took their revenge by building two cottages on the plot they owned in front of Odun Farm, thus blocking the latter's view of the river. But that was a long time ago, and the feud is long forgotten.

~~~~~~~~~~

Odun House is the kingpin of the road - but who was Odun anyway ? "Local hero" is the answer; it was the army of Odun, Earl of Devon, that saw off Hubba the

50

Dane and his marauders over a thousand years ago. The raiding party, whose fleet was moored in the river, had been routed from a fort named Cynuit, and fought their final rearguard on a point on what is now the road between Appledore and Northam.

The Danish chief fell in the battle there and his burial spot was marked by a cairn close to the river. That's the story, and defenders of the local version tell you that Cynuit is clearly Kenwith (which has remains of an old castle) between Northam and Abbotsham, and that the cairn is to be found at Hubbastone, near the great Bidna Yard. The site of the fatal battle is clearly marked, they say, by the memorial stone at the point on the road called "Bloody Corner."

Trouble is, Kenwith was called "Henniborough" and Hubbastone (though it appears as such in one antique map) was apparently called "Whibblestone" until an 18th century antiquarian published his account of the events. Other experts say it all happened up at Countisbury near Combe Martin. Take your pick - nobody has found the cairn, but human bones and ancient coins have been unearthed at Bloody Corner, and the name of Odun has become an immovable feature of Appledore mythology.

Odun House - to get back to the subject - fleetingly links the Torridge with the Thames, for it was here that Jerome K ("Three Men in a Boat") Jerome's father farmed, preached, and mined for silver with varying degrees of success; if he had not accepted a call from the Congregationalists of Walsall, the younger Jerome might have been born here. From serving as the manse and printing shop for the Jeromes, Odun House passed to a master mariner and through other hands, until it was taken over by the District Council and leased to the Trust which runs the North Devon Maritime Museum.

The Museum is a triumph for voluntary effort, even if the District Council did its bit by making the old house available and keeping it sound. If you walk along Odun Road on a winter evening, you are likely to see lights on in the upstairs rooms and hear the sounds of hammer and saw: that's the little group of enthusiasts making new displays and charting the history of the sea and ships along the North Devon coast - and a lot further away, for recent additions celebrate the Armada and the Australian bicentennial.

For all that, the highlight for the younger visitors is the pump in the back garden: the reconstructed kitchen leaps the generations as grannies explain the curious utensils to their grandchildren, then young and old flex their muscles on the pump to draw up the ice-cold water. No wonder the Museum has won a National Heritage award.

One piece of industrial archaeology has been removed from Odun Road with never a nostalgic tear shed for its departure: during the war there was at the bottom end of the car park a large circular water tank all stocked up against German incendiary bombs. Not as fanciful a defence as you might imagine, for the waters round the estuary were training grounds for the Normandy landings. Servicemen by land, air and sea were all stationed here with their air-sea rescue boats, while the local yards turned out minesweepers and motor torpedo boats.

Appledore was a supply and experimental base, and the business of landing men from invasion barges must have seemed comparatively simple alongside the curious devices that were tried out by the boffins of the day. Call at the Maritime Museum to find out exactly what was the purpose of the Grand Panjandrum and why it caused so much terror when it ran amok.

If you have parked in the car park opposite the Museum, you can hardly fail to notice the memorial plaques on the far wall. The car park was once the garden of Odun House, and the plaques mark the last resting place of a variety of household pets. "Sammy" was a much-loved cat, the others were golden retrievers, and there they lie, wrapped up, every one of them, in a fine unused linen sheet before they were brought by wheelbarrow across the road.

She was a great animal-lover, was the lady who buried her pets so ceremoniously, but the occasion when she claimed she had seen a donkey in her garden (behind a six-foot wall and a locked gate) probably owed more to the contents of a bottle than to her fondness for the four-footed kingdom.

Odun Road must be a postman's nightmare: it starts logically enough with no.1, but after that hardly a house has a number, and in less than fifty yards are Odun Hall, Odun Villa, Odun House, Odun Cottage and Odun Grange, which is still regularly addressed as Odun Farm. Finally, there is Bude House, not to be confused with the Bude House less than a hundred yards away down Bude Street.

Appledore - Seagulls

Barrie Payne. 88

APPROACHING THE HIGH

Tea-time in the Parlour

The tide is well up once more, and the water is lapping the wall of the quay.

By the slipway, small boys are crabbing. There's an art to it, and like all artists, they divide into hotly-contested schools. It all hangs - literally - on the bait you use: one school swears by raw fatty bacon, another by squid, a third by stale mackerel, a fourth by limpets knocked off the rocks at Badstep down by the lifeboat slip. It matters tremendously which is right when it comes to the annual crabbing contest, for local honour is at stake, and touring parents have been known to become so swept up in the frenzy of it all as to forget the rule that opens the contest only to teams of four children, each on a marked stretch of the Quay.

Personally, I'm sure that the first real secret of crabbing lies not in the type of bait, but in the size and attractiveness of it. A large swirling tendril-full bundle of anything meaty will attract the waving claws much more readily than a dainty morsel pinned neatly on its hook. The second secret comes later; once you have enticed your crab to catch hold of the bait, and started to raise it ever so gently through the water to the surface - don't hesitate or hurry once it (or they, if your lump of bait is sufficiently seductive) are out in mid-air between the water of the river and the water of your bucket. A steady hand-over-hand pull with no anxious vibrations will swing your captives over the lip of the Quay and into the bucket with the others. Catch enough of them on the big night of the contest and you will win a prize, a sense of achievement, envious glances, and a name in the records of the regatta which runs it all.

And afterwards — be gentle with the crabs. Don't fling the bucket's contents back into the water. Walk down the slip, empty the bucket slowly on to the ground, and let the crabs and the water find their own way back into the river.

~~~~~~~~~~

Here at the corner of the Quay is the little pool known as the Parlour, a right and proper name for a sheltered anchorage. There are always one or two boats lying up here with no particular place to go; in fact one sloop has lain here for as long as I have lived in Appledore without my ever seeing it put to sea. Two-masters (and once the sad remains of a pre-war J class racing yacht) have occasionally moored up here and given the area a touch of instant nostalgia; and when I first returned to Appledore to renew schoolboy holiday memories, the *Golden Hinde* lay here on a summer's evening more golden than any I remembered from teenage years. For a second or two, I was no longer back in the 1950s, but in the 1580s.

Round here the coaling boats used to tie up and off-load. The Appledore lads were always quick to volunteer their help to sweep the decks and replace the hatches, for the loaders always missed a lump or two, and coal was always welcome. As Vernon Boyle puts it:

> "Some of the cottages have flower-beds bordered by large white-washed stones, which close examination will reveal to be lumps of coal. Piracy again: a few bits of coal will not be missed from a cargo, whilst in a garden they look neat and form a useful reserve against hard times."

The closer examination doesn't always reveal coal: some garden paths are bordered by ballast stones, like coral brought from faraway places with strange-sounding names when the ships returned empty-holded to Appledore. Perhaps that explains the three-foot stalactite I found in my garden.

Hard times are still here for the fishermen; even if a bright new trawler, built by Alan Hinks round the point, moors up at the Quay to be fitted out, too often does she have the name of another, distant, port painted on her stern. The serious and commercial fishing has moved on, as have the salmon that once challenged the netsmen here and the rod and line upstream.

That's not to say that fish are no longer landed on Appledore Quay. The signs are on the Quay daily during the summer to let the tourists know when to turn up for what they little realise is a staging of nostalgia. The little boats chug in, the ropes are deftly turned on the bollards, and the trays are lifted up to the quayside for the visitors to make their choice for supper. If you happen to see any squid lying disregarded, buy it: chopped into rings and deep fried in batter, it is an unbeatable delicacy, but it will be disregarded because it is usually only accepted for bait.

Vernon Boyle again:

> The Quay at Appledore is open and breezy, and the narrow streets lead up to interesting old corners. No Quay existed here until 1844, and to understand its existence we must stroll along Market Street, parallel to the Quay and thirty yards inland from it. The houses of Market Street used to have gardens which reached down to the river and ended in massive river-walls, as Dock Cottage and others still do. In 1844 the freeholders of this street clubbed together and built a continuous narrow quay along outside these river walls of theirs. They filled gravel and pebbles in behind the new masonry, and

each house owned its own portion of the Quay. The next stage was to build new houses within the little gardens, thus excellently placed with front doors opening on to the Quay. It is now apparent why the houses of Market Street and the Quay are almost back to back.

The new Quay of 1844 was certainly narrow. It was wavy and rough too. Mothers used to call, when motors rushed along the Quay, "Run, cheeld, run! Put thy arse agenst wall." The Quay masonry was clever, the steps and the piled Quay were picturesque, and there was a flagstaff at Tavern Corner.

Then in 1938 came the Improvers: the surveyors, the engineers, the concrete-mixers, but no masons. Steel rods and slick surfaces were the result and a Quay forty feet wider was run along at the expense of the river."

Time heals, though, and the wartime quay has acquired its own patina, even to the extent of having the repairers in to plug a few gaps in the slipway. A casual glance at the old postcard views in some of the gift shops leads you into a sort of time-warp, until a closer look shows you the scale of the place, and you realise that the distance to the river from those old houses that still look the same (even if the one-time coal cellars have been cleaned up and given rather grander new names) is rather more than it was a century ago.

~~~~~~~~~~

Come down here on an August Saturday evening when the bunting and the lights are up; the Carnival is on its way and the loudspeakers from Tomouth have given way to the live sounds of the Appledore Silver Band. The routine is unchanging: a self-conscious Special Constable, trying hard to pretend that he is on more serious business, marches ahead of the Silver Band and the village fire engine, occasionally murmuring important messages into his radio. The float of honour carries the garlanded Carnival Queen and her equally self-conscious young attendants, and those that follow are the efforts of playgroups and pubs, scouts and school. Everybody knows everybody else, and everybody comes armed with handfuls of coins to lob at their friends and thus swell the pirates' treasure chest, for the Carnival is run by the Appledore Pirates.

~~~~~~~~~~~

If you have walked around the Quay, you must have seen the word "Ope" - ope short for opening. Hardly wide enough to be called streets, but too wide to be drangs (which are for pedestrians only), the Opes lead you to the one time sites of factories and chapels, long since closed down. Who wears separate collars today ? The Duncan and Vincents' factory fell victim to the passing fashion years ago, and only the glove factory in New Street is still in business. Follow your nose and you'll find the real Appledore, the little lanes that lead only to a magic gate in a wall and the point where you have to turn back. On the way, though, you'll pass cottages where the late 20th century has no more effect than the sound of the wind and the surf when your hatches are battened down and the fire is red in the grate.

Only a fragment is left of what must once have been an almost domestic view of the river, turning back from the Bar and looking upstream to the dignity of Tapeley House on one side, a Bidna marsh without the massive hanger-style shipyard on the other, and on up to Bideford.

The trouble is that the old scene is sufficiently similar to the modern one to confuse anyone who tries to explore the past. This was once a creek with a quay facing upstream towards Bideford. Much of the elegant terrace was here: the corner house was once the Custom House, until it became a doctor's surgery in the years before the second World War. The rest of the terrace faced the Narrow Quay, until the far side of the butcher's shop, where a narrow road wound uphill before it petered out into a lane.

On the far side of the creek, other lanes wound over the hillside to other safe moorings. Then in 1856, William Yeo persuaded the owners of the terrace to sell him their frontages to the river, and he built the great Richmond Dry Dock. The view was lost to high dockside buildings, and mouth of the open creek became the tiny Parlour in front of the new patent slipway. The old track up the hill was widened and planted with trees from Yeo's Newfoundland estate which grew so large that the locals eventually named the way Dark Lane.

In 1910 or thereabouts, Dark Lane was turned into the main road, houses in the narrow roads immediately above the creek were removed, and a new road driven round the south side of the creek, leading to Benson's New Quay. At a later stage, the high buildings by Richmond Dock were replaced by a blank wall, and in the 1980s, when the Dock was finally sold off to developers, plans were laid to change the road layout yet again, and there is some slight hope that the view which was closed off in 1856 may be re-opened after 130 years or more. Only slight, because voices are being raised in favour of keeping the old wall, presumably because, being old, it is therefore, a thing of beauty.

~~~~~~~~~~

If Docton House is not the most shameful thing in Appledore, it ought to be. A fourteenth century Cistercian rest house on the way to Hartland Abbey (near where still stands Docton Mill) so it is said, blessed with a Venetian coat of arms and stone mullion windows, it has changed hands several times in recent years, but remains a hulk. It lies sad and neglected in a cobbled yard, blocked from view by a rather ordinary little house.

In some ways, Docton House and the hundred yards or so around it symbolises why Appledore is not another

Clovelly or St Ives. Sure, there are good reasons why we will not - and should not - go whole-heartedly down the road of rampant tourism. Appledore is a working community, not a showpiece for the passing visitor. But the fact, unpalatable as it sometimes seems to be to some, is that visitors *do* pass through the village, and that some of them like to come back year after year. They respect the village and its people, and they wish us well. Yet we welcome their arrival down Marine Parade with a forest of overhead cables, a rusting and derelict shipyard, half a mile of blind stone wall, public toilets that would not be out of place in a pre-war Board School - and we hide our finest house from view. Perhaps, when you see the condition into which its casual owners have allowed it to fall, it may be just as well.

~~~~~~~~~~

Every so often - and not often enough - the Parlour is the grandstand from which to watch a launching. (Strictly speaking, what you are watching is a vessel going off on sea trials, but this is is the public debut of a ship that will have been quietly and privately launched at Bidna weeks before.) Wait for the high tide with your handkerchief at the ready; as soon as it turns, the dead hulk that has been leaning heavily against the quay at Bidna slips sideways (with a little help from the chunky "Lundy Puffin") into the deep channel and suddenly turns into a ship.

Latest of the changelings was a bright red ferry, one of a package deal struck with the ill-fated yard at Sunderland. Complexities industrial and political fouled up affairs to the point where the North East Ship Builders closed down with its last order uncompleted. Appledore gained an order and a couple of dozen Geordie welders to finish the job off. Just to keep boredom at bay, the Bidna yard changed hands and moved into the private sector.

The North-South divide was emphatically breached on the night the ferry was due for her first sea trials. "She's going out at 6.00, and I was the last one off her" announced one of the quartet of Geordies boarding with us. (We had "Susie's sizzlers", while "Jessie's giants" stayed at a guest-house on Marine Parade.) Unusually high tides marked the date and the watchers on the quay's edge were divided by a foot-deep channel of murky water from those on the steps of the quayside houses.

Two hours went by as the crowd grew and the Sunderland lads ran their own ferry service to and from the bar of the *Coach and Horses*. As the light faded, so the humour brightened. A pre-war car rattled through the floodwater - "Hey, that's almost as old as the wife!" cried a Geordie voice. "But it's worth a lot more" returned a Devon one.

Smoke poured from a funnel in the darkness - "that'll be the gennies" ran the commentary. Sparks flared - "They're burning off the gangway, she'll be off soon." Then the current slowed, rested, and began to ebb. The tug moved in and warps began to tighten. "She'll not get far if that little thing has to tow her."

A whooping hoot shattered the night, answered by a ragged cheer from the Parlour supporters club. "She's on the move!" Lights swung round, reflected in the choppy waters, and in total silence, the ferry glided towards us. The cheers grew a little, hankies and scarves were waved - from ship as much as shore - names were called out, and faint cries from midstream hinted that their owners acknowledged the greetings. The siren howled and howled again as the massive red slab slid gently past. Then she was on her way to the Bar, and the little crowd fell quiet.

"Well, Tommy," came a thoughtful question in the accents of the North East, "what's it feel like to build your last ship ?"

SLACK WATER

Evening along Irsha Street

As the tide comes back to the full and the boats bob in the water, their topsides reflected in the lights from cottage windows, we are in Irsha Street.

Why "Irsha" ? Irsha was once the name of a separate riverside settlement which later became West Appledore, but what the word itself means I have no idea. Until recently, West Appledorians were known locally as "West-be-straners", which doesn't throw an awful lot of light on the matter.

This is the spine, the High Street of West Appledore. Time was, when it was as much a main road as the Quay itself, for the original route into Appledore took you straight over the hill now covered by the Riversmeet estate and down Meeting Street to the pool by the church, from where you turned left or right for whichever of the twin villages you sought.

That pool divided more than two sets of houses. Irsha Street is the centre of a community that feels itself to be quite different from the people who live around "Point" - Market Street and the Quay to the passing stranger. In 1868 (the year my grandfather was born, so we're not talking about the dark ages), a feature in "John Bull" described

> "the curious town of Appledore where the inhabitants are as wild and uncivilised a set as any to be found in this part of the kingdom and where, till lately, a stranger could not pass without insult. Shoes and stockings are here unknown luxuries to the

younger portion of the population and the women may be seen sitting outside their doors in the streets working (or more frequently quarrelling) as is seen in the South of Europe."

When I showed that passage to one of my near-contemporaries who was born and brought up here, he commented, "As a boy, I enjoyed regular stone fights on this beach or sand ridge against West gangs." He went on to remark that in past years, much witchcraft was believed to have been carried out in Appledore, adding that his own family was believed to have suffered.

If you want to sort out the witches among your friends, it seems that all you need to do is buy an onion, scoop out the top and fill it up with dragon's blood (which, of course, you can buy from a local chemist); burn the onion, and the first person to call on you thereafter will be a witch – which could prove embarrassing among your neighbours...

If you are tempted to take all this frivolously, let me cite a one-time Appledore neighbour who flatly refused to consider a move to Irsha Street on no other ground than the possible Satanic tendencies of the people who might live next door; or the Appledore man (one among many) who would turn back home and make a fresh start for any journey if his path were crossed by one of a certain group of elderly village ladies.

While I was still absorbing the notion that here in the post-industrial era I counted friends whose family might have been the victims of witchcraft, I came across Jim Butcher's description of Appledore in the days that lay between those two recommendations above –

In my young days Appledore had a reputation for lawlessness. It had the toughest village policeman in the Devon constabulary. He only had one eye but he kept the rule of law intact. To go single-handed into

Appledore on regatta night was to risk a severe beating-up.

A waterfront entrepreneur at Barnstaple was much talked about by the youth of the town because it was said he filled his motor-boat and a converted lifeboat on Sunday mornings when the tide was right with men seeking the delights of the more liberal Appledore ladies down river.

"Trips down the Rhine" was the title of these excursions."

Which reminded me that another local had told me that election nights in his youth were as risky as regatta nights if you were thought to have voted the wrong way, and that the fishermen were only too glad to be over the Bar and out of reach. I told you that we were not talking about the dark ages.

~~~~~~~~~~

Evening is the time to visit Irsha Street. The lights are on in the cottages, but the curtains are not yet drawn, walking through to the lifeboat slip is to pass one intimate stage set after another, and the tourists today are apparently encouraged to be as inquisitive as their grandparents.

But the tastefully lit Irsha Street cottages are not, for the most part, where Appledore folk live. This is the home of the second home, empty or let to temporary residents for the winter, and let out again (at a more profitable rent) to summer holidaymakers when the owners are not themselves in residence. Easter sees the invasion of the big Volvos with the cleaning and decorating gear, and the summer brings the weekly migration in and out of the tiny bedrooms and galley kitchens.

65

Does that matter very much ? The incomers have pushed the prices well out of reach of the locals, and the seaward side of Irsha Street is now worth £10,000 a cottage more than the landward side. But would the young locals in search of a first home really have wanted these cottages in their original state, pokey, damp, in need of rewiring and reroofing, and beyond the respectable world of the 90% mortgage ? And don't the holidaymakers bring business to the shops and pubs of the village ? How many of the old people still living in the unrestored cottages would gladly move into comfortable and secure single-person flats, if only such a thing were to be found in Appledore ?

Behind the scenic frontages of Irsha Street, life can be pretty basic; raw sewage reaches the sea by way of long pipes fitted with valves to ensure that the stuff is not seen emerging until the end of the pipes are decently shrouded under water; when the tides are exceptionally high, the water, with its unsavoury cargo, has been known to surcharge back into the village streets.

I once nearly bought a house in Irsha Street: all seemed suitable, until I shinned down the remnant of a banister into the basement where I found a flourishing buddleia tree directly beneath the kitchen floor. Whatever had been nurturing and feeding it to the size it had reached had no place, I decided, inside any house I might want to live in, and I declined the offer. Perhaps I was being too fastidious.

~~~~~~~~~~~~

Near the middle of Irsha Street, by a narrow slip leading down to some sheltered moorings, is a house that looks as if it were once something a little grander. Indeed it was, for this was the Gaiety cinema, creation of one Mr Hawkins whose cinema generator also ran the electric lights on the Quay, and later the empire of the Thorntons, showing twice weekly on Tuesdays and Saturdays.

Halfway down the aisle was a wider seat, much favoured by the regulars, not for its extra width, but for its position by the door: not even the slightly higher volume of noise of wind and wave made up for the enviable proximity to the cinema's outdoor toilets.

For those who could afford the gallery, there were the seats that came from Sammy Guard's "Pride of the West" coach, and there was the Revd Yewcas Muller with his Blue Bird toffees. The groundlings were a different kettle of fish: "Do be quieeait! You'm like a bliddy circus!" would cry the lady with the lamp. "And you'm the bliddy monkey!" would come the inevitable response.

Twenty-five years ago, tiring of Soho and television, Daniel Farson came home to North Devon to see if he could write. "Twenty-two books later I'm still trying to find out! At least I can succeed in publishing – whether I can write is another matter."

Another writer nearly found a home in Irsha Street, or at least a home for his enormous collection of papers. In 1953, Henry Willamson thought of buying a cottage in Appledore for £350 – "near the pub where the BY (Bright Young) People once haunted, and E. Waugh wrote, in seclusion, *Vile Bodies*." Describing Williamson's plan, Daniel Farson paints a vivid picture of Appledore in both the 50s and the 30s :

"Though little evidence is left, it is true that the Bright Young people came there in the early 1930s: old fishermen relate with relish how they rowed visitors to the yacht anchored in the estuary where the celebrated drug-addict, Brenda Dean Paul, swam naked; the village of Instow, opposite, enjoyed an élite invasion of wealthy lesbians in the summer; while Evelyn Waugh once stayed on Lundy Island for a holiday with friends (the legend persists that either Williamson or Waugh escaped through a pub window in Appledore to avoid a meeting,

but this is a hearsay after fifty years).
When Henry considered the cottage in 1953,
he was saddened by the changes he found in
the village of Appledore - 'Paper, Walls ice
cream cartons, shrieking children. A
polluted estuary; a £1 million electric-coal
station erected just over the water on the
snipe bogs that once were. The Burrows are a
tank ground now.' He was remembering the
estuary from halcyon days, when he was
younger and the landscape fresher."

Perhaps we all do the same. Williamson in the 1950s
reflected on the downward slide from the 1930s. My
generation looks back to those 1950s as the time when
North Devon was undiscovered by mass tourism, weekend
dashes from Bristol were unknown, and day trips took you
no more than 20 miles from home. Perhaps our children
will ask us for stories of how peaceful a place Appledore
could be in those remote 1980s before the Link Road was
opened.

~~~~~~~~~~

If you know where to look - at the semi-derelict length
of red brick wall with two curious hollows in it, just
above the first cottages on the landward side of Irsha
Street - you'll find the last remnant of a local transport
service that dates back further than even the outdated
A361.

Locals still talk of the main road here as "the lines", for
the road is built along the course of a curious hybrid
which went by the grand name of the "Bideford, Westward
Ho! and Appledore Railway". A railway it undoubtedly
was, as the little shunting-style engines pulled carriages
along rails of standard gauge. But it shared Bideford
Quay with everything else that moved, on four legs, two
legs, or wheels; and its carriage design seemed to owe as
much to trams as to more orthodox trains.

The railway was forced by the contours to take a roundabout route to Appledore and back. From Bideford Quay, it ran along what is now the main road as far as Raleigh Hill and the Kenwith Valley, where it swung left and climbed slowly towards Abbotsham village and on to the cliffs, before taking a wide curve into Westward Ho! by the back door and crossing the Burrows to Appledore.

The village mustered no less than three stations, and the railway day-tripper arrived first at Richmond Road Halt, where today's cross-roads lead to the Skern. Shortly after passing the Appledore gasworks, now the Watertown Garage by Hinks' shipyard, one could alight at Lovers' Lane Halt, near the modern lifeboat slip, or stay aboard until the terminus here at the beginning of Irsha Street.

All gone - the rolling stock was shipped out to France in 1917, and like so many other locals, failed to return. The lines were lifted and their track, like so much that once relied on the railway, has been taken over by the petrol and diesel engine. So far as Appledore is concerned, only the back wall of the waiting room, with its two naked chimney-breasts, is left. At least the wall now has a discreet plaque to claim its identity.

The rails here gave way, as they did in so much of Devon, to the roads, and long before "deregulation" came back into fashion Appledore boasted at least three bus services; as well as the ubiquitous National service, villagers could take to the road on Mr Hocking's *"Ensign"* coaches or Mr Hamlyn's *"Brown Bears"*, to say nothing of Mr Guard's *"Pride of the West"* service to and from Watertown, when Mr Guard wasn't running his one-man regatta. Much later, when the free-for-all returned, tourists had their worst suspicions about Devon yokels confirmed when green buses appeared on our roads bearing the legend "This is a Red Bus".

~~~~~~~~~~

Back in the dark ages, all of fifty years ago, anyone showing any curiosity along Irsha Street would certainly - say the locals - have been slated or spat upon. My own contemporaries talk of being apprehensive when they walked there as children. Today's Irsha Street, however, is designed for the curious and the thick-skinned. You'll miss half the attractions if you don't peer through the windows and walk into the tiny courtyards hidden on either side of the road. Everybody sees the Doll's House, with its tiny frontage set back from the pavement, but it isn't everybody who turns off the road and into the courts that provide a front yard for perhaps half a dozen houses literally built into each other's structure in what is poetically called a "flying freehold" - the term covers up the fact that your first-floor rooms will have to learn to fly if your neighbour neglects his ground-floor rooms on which they sit.

Irsha Street cottages, when they come on the market, tend to be described as "fishermen's". No doubt they were, but fisherman is too precise a term for the sailing men of Appledore - some fished, but others crewed, captained, and often owned their own coastal vessels, and others sailed wider seas. Perhaps the only thing they had in common, beyond their respect for the sea, was a highly developed sense of superstition: at least one of them would never let a woman aboard, apart from the laver-gatherers, excused because they were fellow-workers. Others would refuse to venture to sea if they met any of the local witches on the way to their boats.

From our vantage point, it is hard to picture just how many mariners there were in the village a century ago; a roll call from the 1870 directory, emphasises Appledore's reliance on those who went down to the sea in ships. Out of 160 or so tradesman and professional people in the village in that year, over half described themselves as "master mariner", and a further 20 (including a Vice-Consul for Norway and Sweden) earned a living from making ships or parts for ships.

The high Victorian years were, after all, the years of steam travel, by rail or by sea. The "North Devon Historical Guide", published in that same year of 1870, links the tourist and industrial sides of Appledore in rich prose :

"Good Inns and Lodging houses are abundant to welcome strangers who tarry there for cruising and fishing on the rivers Taw and Torridge, for sea-bathing, perambulating or riding on the adjacent Northam Burrows, or occasionally crossing the water to Instow to meet the North Devon Railway Trains, for an excursion to Bideford, Barnstaple, or elsewhere. A Steam Packet, the 'Princess Royal', trading from Bristol to Bideford, calls off Appledore and Instow twice a week, to receive Passengers for Ilfracombe, Lynmouth and Lynton, &c.

The North Devon Lifeboat Institution have 3 Life Boats stationed within the harbour, manned by brave seamen, for which the port is so justly celebrated, as occasion may require. There is also an Agent to the Shipwreck'd Mariners' Society residing here, to grant relief to such seamen as may fortunately survive the 'dangers of the deep', or be rescued from peril by the humane agencies provided for them.

The Torridge and Taw have here their conflux with the sea, which flows in the form of a half-square south towards Bideford, and east in its course to Barnstaple. An extensive Pool is formed by the confluence, whereon Men of War can lay afloat at low water, and large Timber-laden ships to discharge, when circumstances prevent their being taken to the various wharves. Fish is plentiful in both these rivers; Salmon, Cod, Bass, Mullet, Plaice, Soles, Eels, Cockles and

Sprats, are taken at the estuary; Scad, Dace, Lampries, Trout and Salmon, are caught further up these rivers in fresh waters, by fly-fishing or otherwise; thus affording pleasurable and profitable amusement. In addition to the supplies daily netted by the various Fishermen for general sale, as well for the markets on Wednesday and Saturday. Trawlers in like manner arrive with Turbot, Soles, Mackerel, Herrings &c., for those and adjacent markets."

Changed days from the spring times when the salmon fishers "barked" their nets in preparation for the start of a season which gave work to 100 men: changed days, and not entirely for the better. You don't need to go too far back to remember the salmon netting in the Skern pool, or even up by Bideford Bridge; but not any longer. The herring moved on years ago, and the only herring boat you'll see here is up at the Maritime Museum. The salmon have been asphyxiated out of the rivers. Maybe they will come back some day, but nobody is being too optimistic.

EBBING TONIGHT, RISING TOMORROW

Sunset over the Lookout

This is the place for the best view out to Lundy — the puffins' island where rates and licensing laws arrived only in the last few years. No wonder they called it "the Kingdom of Heaven". More pedantic souls link that name to the family of William Hudson Heaven, who bought the island in 1834. It was his son who built the church which stands out so clearly in the view from Appledore, but the last of the family found no pleasure in his earthly paradise, choosing to sell it to the Christies of Tapeley (and Glyndebourne) before emigrating to Australia. Like so many Devonians, however, he came home at the end of his days — in this instance as ashes in a tin that, they say, might have served for golden syrup, left by the postman on a Bude Street doorstep, before sailing in the *Lerina* for burial in the family grave by the elegant old Lundy light.

It was Martin Harman, who ran his island like a real kingdom from 1925, issuing his own coinage and stamps in the currency of the native puffin. Charged with a breach of the Coinage Act, he was fined a token 5 guineas, which must have been covered daily by the sales of the island coins and commemoratives. Since 1968, the island has appropriately been a property of the Landmark Trust.

Lundy was the graveyard for many a fine ship, from Don Guzman de Soto's Armada galleon in "Westward Ho!" to the Edwardian *HMS Montagu*, and the modern lights at north and south end were essential replacements for the older light which too often disappeared into the sea mists that shrouded the island from the view of the ships needing pilots up the Bristol Channel.

73

When Henry Williamson strolled on Woolacombe Sands between the wars, he once saw a couple of cars parked by the beach and complained that all was destroyed – "must nature die wherever man goes on wheels ?" When I first came to North Devon in the 1950s, the cars were counted in their dozens, but we thought things would never change. Now they stand ranked in their hundreds in the pay-and-display stockyards, and a broad new road has cut its irrevocable way westwards.

From the Lookout Cottage (which retains a spy-hole window in its north face), you can see the full circle around the village, even if all is not entirely clear. The view is as symbolic as the one we started from; the sun and the tide come and go, and changes come and go with them, yet somehow things seem to stay much the same.

~~~~~~~~~~

Northam Church tower stands as a landmark to sailors and landsmen alike just as it did when the mother of Amyas Leigh watched her sons cross the Bar to fight in Ireland, to cross the Atlantic, and to defeat the Armada. From here, the Burrows look exactly as they did when Kingsley had young Amyas gaze over them (perhaps from this very point) before running down through the fuchsia-laden hedges and over the pebble ridge to the sea.

> "... then he pauses a moment to look around; first at the wide bay to the westward, with its southern wall of purple cliffs; then at the dim isle of Lundy far away at sea; then at the cliffs and downs of Morte and Braunton, right in front of him; then at the vast yellow sheet of rolling sandhill, and green alluvial plain dotted with red cattle at his feet, through which the silvery estuary winds onwards towards the sea. Beneath him, on his right, the Torridge like a land-lock lake, sleeps broad and bright between the old park of Tapeley and the

74

charmed rock of the Hubbastone, where, seven
hundred years ago, the Norse rovers landed
to lay siege to Kenwith Castle, a mile away
on his left hand; and not three fields away,
are the old stones of 'The Bloody Corner',
where the retreating Danes, cut off from
their ships, made their last fruitless stand
against the Saxon sherriff and the valiant
men of Devon. Within that charmed rock, so
Torridge boatmen tell, sleeps now the old
Norse Viking in his leaden coffin, with all
his fairy treasure and his crown of gold;
and as the boy looks at the spot, he
fancies, and almost hopes, that the day may
come when he shall have to do his duty
against the invader as boldly as the men of
Devon did then. And past him, far below,
upon the soft south-eastern breeze, the
stately ships go sliding out to sea."

~~~~~~~~~~

Follow the compass round a little, and there is the golf
club and the faded Victorian gentility looking down its
nose at Westward Ho! Perhaps the resort centre has
been changed utterly now into a sea of caravans, chip
parlours, amusement arcades and chalets, but it still
seems unable to escape the dominance of Kipling's College
and the tors named after its most famous pupil, and
perhaps the more recent drift towards homes and away
from chalets may restore some of the earlier tone.

~~~~~~~~~~

On down the coastal path, through Peppercombe, saved
from development by the National Trust, and on to Bucks
Mills where almost every home has been sold out of
fishing for holidaymaking instead. The herring and the
limekilns have had their day and departed. Nature, the
moralist might say, then took her revenge by pouring ton
upon ton of unstable cliff over the path to the beach in
mid-season, while poor helpless men could not agree

either on how to remove it or who should pay the bill for its removal.

Clovelly is a white slash down the dark cliff, down which pours a daily torrent of tourists. The RNLI lifeboat there has gone (though the locals are winning the battle to raise funds for a private replacement), and the Hartland light which marks the end of the cliffs before they sweep down to Cornwall flashes automatically now. The coastguard has gone, though the Chivenor helicopter is still - just - here; but the Appledore lifeboats still keep station.

~~~~~~~~~~

Across the straight line of the sea and past Lundy to the other end of the bay. So fierce and so unresolved is the ownership struggle that the maps diplomatically mark this stretch of water as "Barnstaple or Bideford Bay". Your choice of name is settled by whereabouts on its shores you live.

The arm opposite Hartland is Morte - death. An appropriate name and many a sailor has had cause to fear the Morte Stone and the cliffs behind it. One weekend fisherman in recent years stood with his foot jamming open the cockpit hatch while his fellow sailor radioed the Hartland coastguard for help as their little vessel took on water after striking a submerged log. Not until he started to go down with the boat did he realise that his other foot had become tangled with ropes. A strong swimmer, he was able to free his foot before taking several desperate strokes to the surface. The next he knew, he was in the intensive care wing of the District Hospital. The entire rescue was over in minutes; but the new coastguard system, covering the bay from South Wales, anticipates rescues taking longer than before and expects you to have a radio on your vessel: the figure of an hour before rescue has been mentioned. Off Morte a man can die in minutes, never mind a whole hour. Remember the crew of the *Weazle*.

The nearer point is Baggy, with the large Baggy Leap buoy. Croyde's bayful of holiday camps is discreetly hidden from sight up here, and only the slab of the Saunton Sands Hotel, as white and angular as any by-pass motel, breaks into the line of cliffs that lead to Braunton Burrows, a second championship golf club, and the Great Field where Tarka the Otter passed a frozen and dismal winter.

~~~~~~~~~~~

Where the rivers meet, the Bar roars at all stages of the tide: from here you can mark out the path of the buoys that guide all manner of craft through the safety of the narrow deeper channel to the open sea. Down there is Crow Point where the rivers merge and the barges moor for gravel and the lighthouses and chapel once stood; down there a ferry once ran across from Appledore to Crow as the direct route to Braunton, a river trip of no more than a few hundred yards, followed by a walk of a mile or so. We have progressed since those primitive days, and the journey by car is no more than 15 miles.

Across the Taw until recently stood the power station. Only thirty years ago, Henry Williamson complained of its arrival, then it spent some dead and empty years, losing even its last role as a training site. Removing the chimneys did nothing to reduce its evil impact on the view, and only made the building more of a hulk than before, until the demolition men carefully took out the asbestos and took down the walls. "I can remember the outcry when that thing went up", said a neighbour to me on the Quay one morning, "and how much we hated it. Now that it's going, we're all going to miss it. The centre of the view will be so empty."

~~~~~~~~~~~

Veering eastwards and coming upstream, Instow balances Appledore across the river, the twin leading lights marking the direction of the channel to incoming vessels before the pilot takes over control through the shifting passage.   As the sun goes down,   the windows of Instow   blaze   into   fire,   and   from   the   bar   of   the Commodore Hotel, Appledore becomes a silhouette wearing a string of coloured gems as the lights come on along the Quay.

Just as the modern parts of the village were the last to come to light as the sun rose, so   are they   the first to disappear   as   the   sun   goes   down.   The   only   certain lights   are   the   ones   shining   out   to   sea   as   they   have always done; the only sounds will be the ones from the houses and pubs of the village once the holiday cars have driven off for the day.

In the last fading light of the evening, it is easy enough to drift back a century or more to the creekside cluster of   cottages   where   the   only   noises   are   the   splash   of water on wooden hulls, the creaking of ropes, and the roar   of   the   distant   surf.   Exactly   as   once   it   was – exactly, perhaps, as it always will be.

I have heard it said – and I have repeated it here more than once – that Appledore could become another Clovelly. Perhaps it could become another St Ives.   Some people here   would   want   neither.   Many   of   them,   if   they   only knew the sentiment, might shrug their shoulders and echo the   words   carved   on   the   wall   of   the   University   in Aberdeen –

"They Say
Quhat Say They ?
Let Them Say!"

ACKNOWLEDGEMENTS

Cover   The Torridge at Appledore (AEW Lilley, 1918)
                (By kind permission of Mr & Mrs Bruce Woolaway)
Inside front   Appledore in 1754
                (By kind permission of Bideford Town Council)
Inside back   Appledore in 1843
                        (Northam Tithe Map: Diocesan Copy)
                (By kind permission of Devon Record Office!)

p. 4	Chanter's Folly	Tom Andrews
p.10	The Lifeboat House	Tom Andrews
p.30	"La Noroise" at the Quay	Barrie Payne
p.36	St Mary's Church	Tom Andrews
p.44	Docton House	Tom Andrews
p.53	Appledore Seagulls	Barrie Payne
p.54	The Crab that got away	Tom Andrews
p.72	"Snowdrift" at the Cinema Slip	Barrie Payne
p.79	Inner Pulleys Buoy	Tom Andrews

~~~~~~~~~~

I confess to reading at least some of the local books, and am grateful for permission to quote from the following :

"Henry" © Daniel Farson (Michael Joseph Ltd., 1982)

"Tales of the Unexplained in Old Devon" by Judy Chard (Obelisk Press, 1986)

"Devon Harbours" by Vernon Boyle and Donald Payne (Christopher Johnson, 1952)

I am not conscious of quoting from "Appledore, Handmaid of the Sea" by John Beara, but I have used it as the unparalleled reference book on the village, and am delighted that it has reached its fourth reprint.

Printed by Aycliffe Press, Barnstaple